Domestic Violence

How to Map Out an Exit Strategy

Marsha Dean Walker
MSHS, HS-BCP
And
James E. Eastwood
CIS, CFP®

This book is for Tonya Hunter, Sherri Levanti Means, Laura Cowan, Leola Jolly, Edna Sutton, the fallen, the silent screamers and the survivors.

Marsha Dean Walker and James E. Eastwood

Foreword

As the reader proceeds through the pages of this book, there are some issues that are important to keep in mind: the intent of writing about escaping domestic abuse is NOT, in any way, an endorsement of ending committed relationships on a whim, whether those relationships involve marriage, domestic partnership, or any less-formal expression of a couple's commitment to one another. The book also recognizes the universality of domestic abuse, that it is not confined to any social, racial or economic group, and that each incidence of abuse exists in its own unique microcosm, apart from any attempt to generalize the act – violent or not – that is perpetrated. There is no attempt in this book to pinpoint a single, overriding cause of abuse, or even to identify any racial or gender more prone to becoming the abuser. The primary intent is – first and foremost – to be a tool for those who believe they are a victim, to assist them in identifying their position, gain emotional support, and begin to find a positive direction that will help them break the abusive cycle.

Even though there is no distinction between those of greater or lesser financial means who may find themselves victims of domestic violence, it is an undeniable fact that there is a dramatic difference in the resources utilized by those who have a defined strategy for escaping the cycle of abuse, versus those who do not. The first step for many is finding a shelter that will allow them a moment to breathe, the next to contact one or more social services agencies, the choice of contact often based on whether children's needs are involved. The abuse victim can avail himself or herself of many levels of services – local, state and even veterans – depending on their background and level of need. Everything from transitional housing to job preparation and search skills to health care and educational opportunities may be there for the asking, so long as the individual has the awareness that the programs exist and actually ASKS for the assistance. This is the real challenge faced in the writing of this book – helping to build the awareness of how pervasive and damaging domestic abuse actually is, and helping create a pathway for the victim to follow that will lead them to the help they so desperately need. Family assistance is not so much a recommended course of action for domestic violence or abuse victims, as involvement of family and/or friends can actually put into harm's way those who may be least able to deal with an abusive or violent situation. Another critical issue this book must address is the pathway the abuse takes. Often the source of abuse can be traced to an event or series of events that initially create a feeling in the abuser of powerlessness in one environment, only to manifest itself as abuse of another individual in a different environment, where a feeling of control can exist. The abusive supervisor who bullies subordinates may have a home environment that allows them little or no control. In the same way, even a teacher, parent, the driver following too close on the freeway or weaving in and out of traffic, or the person who brings a gun to work, school, or the mall, may have their abusive and violent tendencies traced to an environment where they simply hold no control in their own hands. Their sometimes desperate need to find some shred of control can boil over in an instant and those about them – whether co-workers, family, friends or sometimes complete strangers – can easily find themselves victims of – at the very least –

extreme verbal abuse, and at the worst, violence escalating to the highest levels. While it is beyond the scope of one single book to deal with all causes of abuse and violence, there are definite steps that can be taken which will allow a safe escape from abusive situations. The first step is to gain an understanding of the abuse, to build a plan that will allow the victim to escape, and then follow a strategy that will allow them to keep away from the abusive environment and not fall into a new abusive surrounding. Survival is the first and most important consideration. Much like the difference between cowardice and courage, the survivor is often no less fearful of the abuse they face, they simply do what they must to save themselves, even in the face of that fear.

Marsha Dean Walker and James E. Eastwood

Invictus

Out of the night that covers me,
Black as the pit from pole to pole,
I thank whatever gods may be
For my unconquerable soul.

In the fell clutch of circumstance
I have not winced nor cried aloud.
Under the bludgeonings of chance
My head is bloody, but unbowed.

Beyond this place of wrath and tears
Looms but the Horror of the shade,
And yet the menace of the years
Finds and shall find me unafraid.

It matters not how strait the gate,
How charged with punishments the scroll,
I am the master of my fate:
I am the captain of my soul.

William Henley

Marsha Dean Walker and James E. Eastwood

The Rationale of a Strategy

The life of a relationship can be filled with love, respect, mutuality, honesty and all the emotional components that make for a good partnership. When the partnership is no longer workable, a couple may decide to split and agree to disagree amicably or with animosity.

The life of a relationship can also be filled with the ugliness of power and control and violence. Fear becomes the glue that loosely binds a couple to each other; the fear of violence and verbal abuse. There is the fear of loss – the loss of material things, the loss of inclusion, and the loss of the ability to survive independent of the abuser.

When domestic violence is involved in the disintegration of a relationship, an exit strategy can literally make the difference between life and death. Once the decision to leave is made, secrecy becomes even more paramount than before as does acceptance of the status quo. Nothing can be done to tip a hand or alert the abuser.

An exit strategy gives the abused partner guidelines for safely moving out and moving on. Without it, the risk for harm increases significantly and closes the window of opportunity for a successful transition.

My Story

I can remember being three years old listening to all the noise – yelling, screaming and swearing and the fighting! There were always punches being thrown by the men of the house or men who visited the house at the women of the house. It was cramped quarters at best with a lot of drinking and violence. I used to take it all in like a tiny audience at a grown people's boxing match.

As I got older, I used to hide in the closet behind the clothes with my hands over my ears and rocked back and forth to shut out the sounds. At some point I started taking books to the attic to block out the sounds. I became used to it and accepted it at face value as part and parcel of what it was like to be married. After all, the neighbors all lived that way. I could hear their screams also often followed by an eerie silence. But no one could hear my silent screams when I had my hands tied behind my back and a knife at my throat just because a very sick relative decided it would be fun to torment a little girl.

As a teenager I had my first up close and personal experience with what I later discovered was labeled "domestic violence".

My mother, two sisters, my brother and him, the boyfriend all shared a two bedroom apartment in a very unsavory part of town-far worse than the neighborhood we left.

Mr. Boyfriend and I did not get along. He was an arrogant snot, just four years my senior who played my mother like a well tuned fiddle. Free food, shelter and of course an opportunity to punch or pinch me at will. A blind eye was turned - heaven forbid the boy toy dump his middle-aged paramour and take his leave. That was the first time I thought anything would be better than dying or something far worse.

Back in those days, kids didn't run away - at least not teenage girls - so I ran to a life - a life that included being pregnant, married, on welfare and of course more abuse. It was 1967 and I was 17 years old living an adult life. I blamed myself for the abuse. After all, who knew how to be the perfect wife at 17, so of course, everything I did was wrong. He controlled with ultimatums, a loud voice, raised fists, isolation and starvation.

It took me five years to "see the light" or maybe I just grew up, but for whatever reason, I left. At 22 I was a little more prepared, except I had two kids to support. I also had a job so my "exit strategy" was a little better thought out and executed. But apparently the lesson didn't take because once again I ended up in another abusive relationship; this time more verbal and controlling. I pretty much bought peace for the duration - eight years worth. Money was the end all, be all - mine that is. I had a couple more kids and even survived being raped by a co-worker. Empathy was not on the menu. Missing a day of work was not an option, so life went on.

Every night when I went to sleep, my purse was dumped, my clothes sniffed and my dresser drawers rifled. Every payday he was there to "pick up" my check before it was in my hand good. I usually ended up with no lunch money. His father physically abused his mother and his brother physically abused his wife. That was the way it was.

I came home from work one day and was pinned against the closet door with a hand around my throat and a derringer pointed at my head. I was barely 30 years old and with no exit strategy in place, I left. I left my house and I left my kids because I had no place to take them. In my mind, my safety was paramount and I would come back to get my kids the next day.

John Steinbeck once wrote about the best laid plans of mice and men often go awry - and so needless to say, I didn't get my kids. They grew up thinking I had abandoned them. I immediately filed for divorce and went on with my life. But I paid such a high price to learn the value of a well thought out, well organized domestic violence exit strategy.

MDW

THINK

Marsha Dean Walker and James E. Eastwood

Chapter One
What Is Domestic Violence?

Whenever the term "domestic violence" is used, immediately images of a woman with a blackened eye or a man with a raised fist are the first things that come to mind. Their stories are first-hand accounts of physical, emotional and/or psychological torment. They are recollections of the irrational behaviors of seemingly insanely angry people.

Domestic violence falls into two categories - criminal and non-criminal. Criminal behavior includes physical contact such as striking, kicking, biting, sexual abuse and certain forms of intimidation such as stalking, computer hacking and criminal isolation such as being locked in a garage, a basement or an attic for periods of time The assault and battery behavior provides obvious proof of abuse. Non-criminal behavior includes economic deprivation such as disallowing a spouse or intimate partner the opportunity for gainful employment, interrupting the work process by making excessive phone calls and unannounced visits to the workplace and withholding and/or controlling access to family finances - such as doling out an allowance or failure to inform the whereabouts of family assets.

Further examples of non-criminal behavior is restricting access to friends or other social contacts, shadowing, restricting the use of the telephone by securing phones in a locked area and/or removing telephones from the home when the abuser is away.

The scope of domestic violence is far more reaching than the black eye or the raised fist. It not only includes spouses, ex-spouses, current intimate partners, ex-partners, parents and children, but impacts on friends, neighbors, co-workers and innocent bystanders who witness the violence.

Statistical Breakdown of Domestic Violence

As a person involved in an abusive relationship, numbers mean nothing. You feel alone in your pain and isolation. You realize there are others enduring the same abuse or worse, and it doesn't matter. But it does matter. The following statistics serve as further incentive to map out an exit strategy and leave the situation.

- One in every four women will experience domestic violence in her lifetime (Tjaden, Patricia et al., 2000), and females who are 20-24 years of age are at the greatest risk for intimate partner violence (U.S. Department of Justice, 2006).

- In 2005, 389,100 women and 78,180 men were victimized by an intimate partner.

These crimes accounted for 9 percent of all violent crime. (Shannan M. Catalano, 2005).

- The majority (73%) of family violence victims are females: 84% were spousal abuse victims and 86% were victims at the hands of a boyfriend (U.S. Department of Justice, 2005).

- One study found that women who have experienced any type of personal violence (even when the last episode was 14 to 30 years ago) reported a greater number of chronic physical symptoms than those who have not been abused. The risk of suffering from six or more chronic physical symptoms increased with the number of forms of violence experienced (Christina Nicolaidis et al., 2004).

- In 2003, lesbians, gays, bisexuals, or transgender people experienced 6,523 incidents of domestic violence; 44% were men, 36% women and 2% transgender (National Coalition of Anti-Violence Programs, 2004).

These are just a few examples of how pervasive domestic violence is in the United

States. It also raises the question of why people remain in abusive relationships.

Chapter 2
Why People Stay

Fear. No matter how bad things seem, for many victims of domestic violence any change from the status quo creates fear and trepidation, and for them, routine abuse has been rationalized. The victim in some cases feels the abuse is justified as they blame themselves for their circumstances. To leave the relationship means being overwhelmed by the unknown and suddenly navigating the waters of life alone.

For other victims, the fear of losing face, status and ostracism from family and friends is a fate worse than the abuse. This is especially true for male victims of intimate partner abuse. Ray is a prime example of how this scenario plays out.

Ray's Story

Ray was a career soldier stationed in West Germany with his wife of nearly 30 years. He was a master sergeant with supervisory duties and responsibilities. He was easy going, likeable and well respected by the men he worked with. When anyone visited their military housing unit, the first thing they noticed was a 2 x 4 piece of wood nailed down the middle of the front door indicating the door had been kicked in at some point.

Gertrude, Ray's wife was the exact opposite of Ray. She was loud and coarse and often times profane. She loved to argue and nit-pick. She also physically abused Ray. One Saturday evening prior to leaving for a night out with the boys Ray decided to pour himself a drink. Gertrude entered the kitchen, took out a bowl of ice and began chipping at it with an ice pick.

Suddenly without notice Gertrude took the ice pick and rammed it full length into Ray's right bicep. As Ray removed the ice pick Gertrude fled into the bedroom where she began pitching armloads of Ray's suits into a bathtub filled with water. Ray bandaged his arm, dressed and left the apartment.

Several hours later there was a knock on the door, Gertrude answered it and Ray took his fist and knocked her to her knees. He then took a dining room chair and broke it across her back. As she lay in pain on the floor, he wrapped the belt to his leather coat around her throat and began dragging her through the house.

In the course of the physical altercation, Ray's shirt was ripped off revealing several old healed scars on his back and his chest. A short time later, the MP's arrived, kicked the door open and transported them both to the dispensary.

The next morning Ray went to work as always, spit-shined boots slung across his shoulder and Twinkie in his hand. Ray did not report the abuse and the report from the dispensary remained in a locked file.

The sole intent of an abusive partner is to exert excessive power and control over a partner by physical means or emotional manipulation. Contrary to popular belief, most abusive partners are not sick or emotionally unwell. The abuse itself is a collection of learned behaviors and manipulative strategies used to subordinate a partner. These behaviors can include threats of suicide or taking children away from the abused. These behaviors can be part of a multigenerational belief system such as a long standing family history of abuse and submission. Witnessing abusive behavior as a young child or during the adolescent years can go hand in hand in creating a failure mentality.

Failure Mentality - Many abuse victims remain in relationships with their abusers due to failure mentality. This negative system of behaviors serves to create a negative identity and a loss of self esteem – the "poor pitiful me syndrome".

Victimization caused by domestic violence doesn't make a person weak. Embracing negativity is what weakens the spirit and fosters hopelessness. There are five components of a failure mentality; negative self talk, negative role modeling, paining behaviors, social and familial ostracism and incompetence.

Through negative self-talk such as "This is all my fault. I deserve it for being so weak", or "I can't do any better and I could do a lot worse", or "I seem to have no control over my own life. The problem is too large for me", the victim surrenders control of their life.

Negative role modeling is acceptance of abuse grounded in family history. "My mother and my grandmother went through the same thing and they survived it all and kept our family intact so I guess I can do it too."

Paining behaviors are the ultimate displays of enhanced denial of the severity of the situation and make excuses for not taking positive life-saving measures. Statements such as, "I'm too depressed to deal with it. " I am too embarrassed to make any changes." "I'm sick." "I will just tune out and it won't hurt so badly."

No one likes to be excluded and fear of ostracism is one of the main reasons victims convince themselves that they can handle it. They convince themselves that people won't like them anymore or that certain members of their family will consider them weak and pathetic and cut them off. They believe they will be abandoned by many of the meaningful people in their lives.

Another term for incompetence is disbelief. The victim begins to question whether they can ever regain control and manage their lives again.

Love. It is impossible for non-abused outsiders to understand the pull of strong emotions experienced by people in abusive relationships. One of the strongest is love. Initially the love was warm, inclusive, and respectful of the individual. At some point and in "plain sight" of the abused, it became obsessive, domineering, jealous and a redefinition of partner roles. It became an outwardly physical expression of ownership and a total denouncement of the individual.

The abused individual becomes a pawn of the abuser - sexually, emotionally and psychologically. This behavior is often exemplified like Nancy's story.

Nancy's Story

Nancy is a 30 something married white female with two kids under two. While on a family shopping trip to Wal-Mart, she attempts to place a package of meat in the shopping cart. Her husband angrily grabbed her wrist and severely admonished her as he reminded her that her function was strictly as a tag-a-long for the kids. She was not allowed to impact in any way on what items went into the shopping cart.

For victims like Nancy, the pain, belittling and grandstanding aggressiveness is a power play designed to keep her in her place. Nancy knows that at some point the anger will subside and the "love" phase or the honeymoon phase where her husband is extremely loving and caring as if nothing happened will come into play. This restores her hope that things may turn around and this she becomes further ensnared in the abuse cycle.

Loss - In violent relationships, the abused rationalizes the behaviors and any thoughts of leaving are tempered with the loss of companionship on "good days" and the loss of financial support. It is the fear of limited financial options and the ability to meet the basic needs of survival that somehow justify the abuse.

Religious beliefs and cultural beliefs-

Culture is closely tied to an individual's religious beliefs and practices, and abuse notwithstanding, many abuse victims are motivated to remain in abusive relationships based on religious principles and expectations. This is especially true in the case of marriage. Every option from pastoral counseling to traditional marriage counseling to simply "living with it" is the only viable options. The family is to be kept intact at all costs.

Divorce can be cause for ex-communication from several religious institutions and/or the need to present before a tribunal to obtain an annulment before being allowed to remarry in the Catholic Church. That stigma of social and familial exclusion is more unacceptable than the abuse.

Chapter Three
The Consequences of Remaining In an Abusive Relationship

The personal emotional toll of remaining in an abusive relationship is incalculable. Every aspect of your daily routine is altered. Your perception of self, thought processes, and interpersonal communications are all designed to feed into the abuse cycle. A victim exposed to prolonged exposure to domestic violence lives in a constant state of fear, anxiety, helplessness, hopelessness, self loathing, depression, embarrassment and become hypervigilant or unable to just wind down or relax. Most victims are always guarded, waiting for the next round of abuse and terrified that someone outside the house will discover the truth.

If the abuse is severe enough to warrant a visit to an emergency room escorted by the abuser, the victim most likely will sit idly by as the story of the "accident" is explained to hospital personnel. Chronic abuse results in chronic physical complaints and a general feeling of unwellness and fatigue which can lead to Posttraumatic Stress Disorder.

Children who witness ongoing domestic violence experience fear at the possible loss of a parent. Shame and guilt at the possible role they play in the violence causes them to experience confusion and anxiety at having to choose sides as well as the fear of being injured if they confront the abuser. Older children may experience anger and depression as they try to shut it all out. Cutting school, suddenly acting out, going back and forth between aggressiveness and passivity, lying and exhibiting age inappropriate behaviors are all consequences of prolonged exposure to a life of violence. Many children become involved in role reversal where they become the caregivers to the abused parent.

One of the direst consequences is the perpetuation of a multigenerational belief system where abuse is viewed as the norm in an intimate family relationship. The longer an abused person remains in a relationship, the louder the message that abuse is an acceptable behavior.

The ultimate consequence of remaining in an abusive relationship is death, either at the hands of the abuser or self-imposed.

If ever there was justification for an exit strategy, it would be the safety and emotional wellness of you and your children. When it comes to domestic violence, sanity takes precedence over sanctity at all costs.

Anna's Story

Anna was raised to believe that marriage was a lifelong commitment and that no matter how bad the bad got, there was never a good reason to leave the relationship and this was especially true if children were involved.

During her fifteen year marriage she was beaten repeatedly by her husband, suffering a miscarriage and a broken ankle at one point. Each incident that required a trip to the hospital was summarily explained away by her being "accident prone" or unfocused.

Her daughters witnessed several years of abuse and the older one began to display signs of regressive behavior. When she raised the possibility of a divorce her husband dislocated her shoulder and threatened to take her children if she reported the incidents of physical abuse and one day while he was at work she took the girls and fled the house.

Anna represents a new group of urban squatter. Displaced from her home she and her two young daughters pose as patients in the waiting area of a busy inner city hospital emergency room. All of their belongings are secured in a black plastic garbage bag in a collapsible shopping cart.

Every morning at shift change, Anna awakens her children and hustles them off to a restroom in a remote part of the building so they can wash up, change clothes and get prepared for school.

After walking them to school Anna spends time at a library, a laundromat and panhandling to get enough money to feed herself and the girls their daily dinner of hot dogs from a cart vendor.

She feels that the hospital is a safe environment until she can find suitable housing and feel assured that her husband is no longer searching for her. Anna feels that if she asks for help she and the children will be separated or if she goes to a battered women's shelter her husband will find her and force her to return to the abusive environment.

Chapter Four
Getting Prepared Emotionally

Now that you have had time to think about what domestic violence is, the cause and non-cause and effect of victimization, you are beginning to understand the necessity for an exit strategy. Now is when you begin to think like a survivor instead of a victim.

For the most part your role in the domestic violence scenario has been that of a hostage and the negative "truths" of your abuser have caused you to become multi-dysfunctional. Now it is time to do some personal hostage negotiation with yourself by becoming emotionally detached from the abuser and emotionally distanced from negative events of abuse.

Instead of giving in or trying to dismantle the feelings and actions of your abuser – the betrayal, the disrespect, the deliberate infliction of emotional and physical pain and your own feeling of powerlessness, you have to learn the difference between thought and feeling.

It is never easy but emotional cutoff is a way of managing the unresolved emotional attachment to the abuser. It is time to write your own truth - beginning with the following survey:

- Are you willing to take charge of your life instead of living as a perpetual victim and realize nothing is beyond your control?

- Do you accept the fact that self-defeating attitudes are based on the faulty belief systems and logic of your abuser?

- Are you willing to control your environment?

- Can you learn to deny the existence of people who make your life miserable?

- Are you strong enough to disarm your abuser by redefining your reactivity to abusive events?

- Do you have so little belief in your own ability to execute an escape action plan that you are willing to die as a result of your own sense of powerlessness?

- Can you enjoy life and function better as a parent and employee without the stress and anxiety of domestic violence?

- Can you recognize the fact that you are no one's property or an emotional, psychological or physical whipping post?

- Can you eliminate all negative transactions with your abuser?

- Do you realize that you are responsible for meeting your own needs on your own terms?

- Do you want to die miserable at the hands of your abuser?

If you answered 'yes' then you are ready to accept and embrace your new role as a survivor and now you are ready to move onto the next phase of planning your exit strategy.

Chapter Five
Goals, Objectives and Outcome

An exit strategy in and of itself is a form of intervention. As a survivor, you are committed to interfering with or disrupting the outcome of your life by creating a plan of action.

The first step is creating ***goals*** for outlining and defining the path of the exit process and clarifying the purpose.

- Become more attuned to the process of coping through positive statements.

- Provide a safe non-threatening means to leave the abusive situation.

- Reduce the effects of the physical and/or emotional abuse by creating a sense of empowerment.

- Creating a financial management program to facilitate the exit and sustain your new life.

- Assuming greater personal responsibility by becoming more self-directed and more self-accepting.

- Engaging in self-determined decision making to no longer play the role of the victim.

- Developing an internal source evaluation and becoming more trusting of self.

- Researching available community resources.

- Learning your rights as a victim and seeking relief through the judicial system.

The ultimate objective of the exit strategy intervention is to decrease the traumatic symptomatology associated with intimate partner abuse. Secondary objectives include safety issues, family self-sufficiency and possible prosecution of the offender. The outcome will be decided by how determined you are to abandon the role of victim and embrace the role of survivor.

Chapter Six
Becoming More Attuned to the Process of Coping Through Positive Self-talk

In the past your abuser controlled your emotional, physical and psychological wellness. Their need to control became your anxiety, your fear, your nightmares, your headaches, stomachaches, your depression, your hopelessness. You bought into the negatives and became your abuser's truth. That was the victim mentality.

As a survivor you are re-establishing your self-esteem by becoming an active listener rather than a passive bystander. You begin to develop a heightened awareness of nonverbal messages and begin to find creative ways to sidestep some of the negative events. This not only buys you precious time, it is key in creating a success identity and reclaiming total control over your own life.

When you become more involved in the process of creating a success identity you begin to reflect on the paining behaviors and make a conscious decision to move away from them.

Here are a few positive self-talk statements that will help you in the process:

I will create a success identity.

I will reclaim total control over my own life.

I will display strength, responsibility and self-discipline.

I will eliminate all paining behaviors - depression, anxiety, body aches.

I will exhibit honest and truthful role modeling.

I will respect my children and not allow them to be used as bargaining chips.

I will not sacrifice my health or happiness for the sake of an image based on the opinions of others.

Chapter Seven
Making Sense of the Dollars and Cents

Traditional financial planning as it has come to be recognized through its evolution over the past several decades involves gathering information about the resources an individual or family has available to them, and then mapping out an action plan that matches those resources – income, savings, retirement accounts, and property – to the needs outlined over both the short and long term. This kind of planning can be incredibly helpful to people in all social and economic levels, but for practical purposes, it is available only to those people who have the means to pay planning fees ranging from perhaps $75 or $100 per hour on the low side, to as much as several hundred dollars per hour. As is even more common, those having assets of sufficient quantity to generate ongoing management fees or up-front commissions that make them attractive to traditional advisors are offered the planning service free of charge. Not only is planning readily available to these individuals and families, but there is significant competition among traditional advisors for the ready supply of prospective planning clients.

For the "traditional planning client", changes in the economy or moving from full employment to retirement may dictate a change in lifestyle, but for those belonging to the upper middle class and above, the changes simply mean a shift from the individual at work to the money at work. The lifestyle change, if any is needed, may mean little more than deciding whether to keep the vacation home or sell it – keep a second (or third) car or get rid of it, and those individuals are rarely forced to decide such matters arising from any need to raise cash. They never face the fear held by their low-income counterparts of getting to the checkout counter and not having the cash to pay for what's in the cart, or worse yet, having a check or credit card denied and be forced to leave empty-handed.

The middle and upper-middle-class, despite having financial resources that can act as a buffer against economic upheaval, are in no way immune to the domestic violence in any of its forms outlined earlier, and having an action plan to escape abuse transcends all social barriers. Consider the abused spouse who has lived comfortably, but never had access to the family's bank or investment accounts, either by choice or because their partner has maintained firm and exclusive control. They may have no idea what financial resources are available to them should they find the situation at home has become intolerable, or worse yet – life threatening, and they may be far less experienced than their less-financially-fortunate counterparts when it comes to making ends meet with little or no ready cash.

For those individuals, the fear level they face when considering an escape from their abusive environment may be far greater than that experienced by someone who regularly deals with financial crises. One of the first steps an upper-middle-class person will need to take when considering an escape from abuse will be to assess those resources that exist in their community, and whether they have access to funds that will allow them to "go it alone" – generally engaging the aid of an attorney or other professional who can assist in getting them moved into alternate housing, contact social services agencies, and begin the process of assessing the need for a permanent separation from the abuser. This is where all abuse victims begin to look the same, regardless of their social or economic standing: an abusive partner – one who's capable of handing out regular doses of physical or emotional torment – is certainly capable of rendering bank accounts and credit cards useless, either by emptying a joint account or cancelling credit cards once they become aware their partner is attempting to escape. The purpose the abuser has here is twofold; prevent the partner's escape by controlling access to finances, and if the escape has taken place, force an unconditional return as a means of covering up the abuse – "capping the spill" so to speak.

For the person of limited financial means, escaping domestic abuse takes on an air of near-impossibility, unless the victim gathers every shred of information on the programs that exist to aid victims of abuse and violence. Generally speaking, the local office of Children and Family Services is the first contact if there are young children that may need protection and assistance. Most communities have domestic violence hotlines or websites that can offer immediate assistance, and can refer the victim to a shelter and to counseling services. The next step is to get help finding transitional housing, as shelters are generally noisy, overcrowded, and may not be the right environment to be in when formulating the long-term decisions that must be made if the victim is to remain safe.

Safety and survival are the most critical considerations when escaping abuse. If the abuser has a pattern of violent or unpredictable behavior, the victim may have to leave with little or no warning – forced to leave behind all clothing, furniture and personal belongings. First and foremost: there is NOTHING a person owns that is worth dying over – NOTHING that cannot be replaced…except their life and the lives of those they care for. This brings up the second consideration of safety and survival: Don't go where the abuser will find you. They will know where your friends and relatives live, and that will be the first place they go to look for you. Don't put others is danger for the sake of convenience! Even if the abusive partner doesn't own a weapon, if they build sufficient rage, they will find one and use it either to threaten or cause harm. Never assume that an abuser who has not been violent will not ever become so. If they have a consistent pattern of abuse, it can easily take a violent turn once their abusive behavior has been revealed. They may rationalize that since their victim has escalated the situation by exposing their behavior, they, in turn, are justified in raising the bar to include violence at the next confrontation.

Chapter Eight
Introducing the Financial Strategy

It is one thing to advise an escape to safety, and quite another to actually take the action needed to escape. For someone on a sinking ship, it may be an easy choice to leap into the sea. Why, then, do so many choose to remain on that same ship and drown as it goes under? Why do some cower in a closet when the home is on fire, only to be overcome by smoke and perish, when safety may have been mere steps away? Ships have mandatory lifeboat drills, and schools have fire drills, just to make everyone prepared in the event – however remote – that disaster may strike. Families are encouraged to make and practice an escape plan in the event of fire in the home. It is all done in the name of survival, and in every case, there is some kind of plan in place to make survival not only possible, but likely.

Planning is the key to being a survivor rather than a victim. Since every case of domestic abuse is unique, the way an escape plan is formulated and the amount of work necessary to implement it will also be unique to the individual's circumstances, personal as well as financial. In this section, though, it is already assumed that the need to escape domestic abuse is clear, so the focus is on the financial strategies that must necessarily be mapped out before one can successfully escape.

The first step in putting together any plan of action is to take an honest look at your personal starting point. As the old saying goes, you will never be able to decide what direction to take if you don't know where you are now. Regardless of your financial situation, you will first need to determine what you will need for income. Think in terms of the things you NEED, not the things you WANT. Unless you have access to funds, think of shelter, food, clothing, and keep it to that. You may have special needs such as medications, and those, too, come under the heading of needs. If you are a smoker, or you like to drink, those are wants, and have to be put at the bottom of the financial list. If you have a job, you may have to take time off if you can, and you may need to let your boss or supervisor know the reason you will miss work. Again, no job is worth your life. You can always get another job.

Expenses for the things you *need* are called committed expenses – things you must have for survival. Any expense you have because you *want* it is a discretionary expense. In good times these are the "mental health" expenses – treating ourselves to nice things, going out to dinner, going on vacation. Survival stays ahead of mental health until the crisis has passed.

Once you have the list of your committed expenses, it's time to look at where you will draw your income. If you have a joint savings or checking account, you may not feel you have the right to take what's there, even if it is rightfully half (or more) yours. If you don't withdraw what is rightfully yours, your abusive partner will almost certainly withdraw *all* the funds once they discover your plan to escape, cutting you off from one of the lifelines you may need. The same goes for savings accounts. If it is a joint account, take your half. Also, if you have an account in your name, never assume it is safe from an abusive partner.

Banks have been known to allow withdrawals by non-account-holders in some circumstances, so don't take the chance your account is guaranteed secure. If you have a credit card in your name only, use it for emergencies, but keep in mind that any amount charged to it will have to be repaid, and at additional cost.

Cash reserves are just that – cash for immediate needs and emergencies. Once again, unless you are one of the lucky few with serious money reserves, your ability to generate income for more than a few days on your cash reserves is doubtful at best. It will be necessary to determine, as soon as possible, what amount you will be able to get from the various public assistance resources, including help with utility bills, food stamps, and some form of monthly cash stipend. There will be some reading this who believe they should never stoop to taking "welfare", and those holding this belief are to be congratulated, while at the same time they must be cautioned. Remember, this is all about planning not only your survival from abuse, but your ability to STAY safe. That means staying AWAY from your abuser. That means not finding in a week or two, perhaps more, that you have run out of ready funds and decide to take the chance that the situation at home has cooled to a safe level. If the situation warranted your escape in the first place, all that has happened during your absence is that your abuser has had the opportunity to build their anger. They may have had no outlet for the feelings that have festered during that time, and you may be walking back into an extremely dangerous environment!

All this comes down to the most critical element of financial planning, and that's building your cash reserves. This is why it's vitally important to be stingy with your ready cash reserves when you first leave, and why it's equally important to take any and all help that's offered as soon as you can get it. You may not know how long the help will be there, and you may not know what expenses may come that you hadn't expected. ***Rule #1:*** Keep a reserve of cash to cover at least a full month of your out-of-pocket committed expenses – food, housing, utilities – the things you *must* have. If you are able to bring in more income than your committed expenses in any month, don't think of it as time to add discretionary spending on top of your committed expenses, think of it as a way to build your cash reserve, working toward two, then three months of committed expenses set aside. ***Rule #2:*** It doesn't matter what you earn on cash reserves. More important, as Will Rogers once said, is the return OF your money, not the return ON your money. Too many people worry about the difference in rates of return on savings. To put it into perspective, if you kept even an average of $1,000 in a savings account that offered an additional ¼% over your current rate, the extra earnings would add up to $2.50 over an entire year. If the account had any additional fees or less ready access to your cash, or was at a bank less convenient to get to, what is that extra $2.50 per year worth now? It is the return OF your money, not the return ON it. Cash reserves should be easy to get to, have no penalties for withdrawal, and be SAFE. This brings up another consideration: cash reserves are not the same as cash. Cash can be *taken*, and is nearly impossible to replace once it disappears. Banks, as we've discussed earlier, are secure, but only if you have given them written instructions that you are the only authorized person that can use the account. One problem with keeping all your reserves in a bank is getting there when you need to access cash. A safe and convenient alternative is a pre-paid debit card. Unlike a credit card, the entire balance in a debit card could be withdrawn by a thief if the card is stolen, so it is not a good idea to keep a higher balance than you need for planned expenses. You can always transfer funds to the card as needed to re-fill the available amount, thus the recommendation of a pre-paid card vs. a card linked directly to a bank account. The other advantage of a debit card is your ability to make a purchase and get cash back if you need it. Unlike going to a bank ATM machine, there is no fee charged by the store for the cash you get, and you can access small amounts to cover additional purchases where the debit card may not be an appropriate payment method.

Here is where we get to ***Rule #3:*** Always be vigilant about your spending, and always be totally honest with yourself about whether every purchase you make is a necessity. This may be uncharted territory for many who have never been given the freedom to make their own choices, but take the opportunity given to you and enjoy it! A big part of successfully escaping domestic violence is taking advantage of the personal growth that will come as you take full responsibility for yourself. Right after cash reserves on the scale of priorities comes planning your income. Here you need to take that honest look at what you have and what you need, and see where the income can be generated. Every source has to be counted – your cash and bank accounts, your longer-term savings, your income (full or part-time), and your retirement accounts, if any. This last item is the one most often overlooked when it comes to planning the escape from abuse. Everyone has heard how critical it is never to dip into a retirement account, but once again, we're talking about planning your survival as the first priority. Not to be mean about it, but that comes way before your plans for long-term comfort and security. Like any other piece of property you may own, a retirement account can be replaced. It may take time, but it CAN be replaced….you can't!

Chapter Nine
Understanding the New Financial Rules

There are some rules the Internal Revenue Service put in place that you need to be aware of, that will make it a lot easier to use a retirement account for planning your income. One rule allows what the IRS calls "equal periodic payments" from an IRA account, even if you haven't reached the age of retirement. It may not create all the income you need, but you can get at your money without paying any early withdrawal penalties, and since the monthly amount you get is predictable, it will go a long way in helping you work around the amount of income you need to bring in. If you need $500 every month to meet your committed expenses, for example, and your retirement account will generate periodic income of $300 each month, then at least you know what you need to bring in from some other source.

If your account isn't big enough to generate income under this rule, don't shy away from the idea of simply cashing in your account. Depending on what other income you have, you may owe some tax – even some penalties for withdrawing from the plan early – but your survival is always more important. Get some help with these ideas! Your bank usually has someone in the branch that can tell you what the rules are covering various types of retirement plan withdrawals, and that should keep you from getting into tax trouble. OK, now we get to ***Rule #4:*** Don't be afraid to get a second opinion. Just because someone sits behind an impressive-looking desk in a bank or investment company office, even if they may know more than you do, never take it as gospel that they have all the answers. They may be motivated partly by helping you, and partly by (OH, how terrible!) feeding their families. People offering planning solutions, whether through a bank, investment brokerage, insurance agency, or independent advisory group, expect their advice to generate some sort of income for them either directly or through their company. Just so you know, and despite what you may have seen on TV, are no specific advantages or disadvantages when it comes to the quality of the advice you get vs. the way an advisor gets paid (commissions, hourly or asset fees, or a flat rate). There may be cases of advisors working "pro bono" (for free), and it may be worth your time to contact the Financial Planning Association for a referral to an advisor who offers pro bono services to those having little or no income (www.fpanet.org). The quality coming from an advisor affiliated with the FPA will be consistent, and probably higher than you will get from the local bank. This is only one alternative, though, as you may have to get to the advisor, rather than he or she coming to you, and getting to another part of town is a cost in time, not to mention the travel expense.

Your income needs will change over time, and hopefully so will your ability to generate income from sources other than your money at work. An advisor can be a great source of ideas for generating the most income from your money, but ultimately the responsibility for income comes down to you. You may be in a committed relationship that seems to be moving in a strong, positive direction, but circumstances can change, and you may find yourself in a position where you are on your own, and your ability to earn is entirely dependent on what you bring to the table. ***Rule #5:*** Never turn down the opportunity to pursue your education and build your workplace skills. The only thing you have that can NEVER be taken from you is your knowledge. It is and will be more precious to you throughout your life than anything you will ever own. Whether your life follows a continuing path of peace or takes a turn that puts you in the path of domestic violence, your knowledge and skills will still be there. This is what will make you a true survivor!

Chapter Ten
A Final Note on Cash Reserves

Before we completely leave the subject of cash reserves, let's take a few moments to discuss what types of accounts can be cash reserves. The pre-paid debit card is one, free checking accounts banks offer is another – no fees for either. A savings account is yet another, but make sure there are no minimum balance requirements – you don't want to suddenly find fees are eating away at your money simply because you don't have enough on deposit to have them waived. Only if you have managed to build your reserve above the three-month level should you consider adding a certificate of deposit to the mix. This type of account will have higher earnings, but only because the bank knows they have your money for three months, six months, a year or more. To get at it earlier, you lose part or all of the earnings, so it is best to "ladder" the maturities (set up a three month, six month, and twelve month certificate) to match your need for available cash. Another cash reserve that can be considered is the cash value in a life insurance policy. This is NOT a good place to build cash reserves short-term! Your net earnings will be less than zero for up to five years or more. If you already *have* a life insurance policy, find out if it has a cash value, and if it does, keep it in mind as a part of your ready cash reserve. Keep in mind, too, that only the *owner* of the policy can get access to the cash – protection for you if you own your policy, but restrictions preventing your access you if your abusive partner is the owner.

A few words about moving up to longer-term cash reserves: A long-term cash reserve is the same as an investment account. The differences in short-term vs. long-term are the earnings you can expect, the risks you take, and the fees collected by the company holding the account. All three are higher as you move farther out on the investment limb, so just bear in mind that we will not spend any time discussing investment accounts. Our purpose is to help you escape and to survive. Taking on additional risks of *any* kind – especially with your reserves – is a *bad idea*, and will almost certainly work against your strategy. Keep it simple….you will have ample opportunity to build wealth when your life becomes more settled.

Traditional financial planning as it has come to be recognized through its evolution over the past several decades involves gathering information about the resources an individual or family has available to them, and then mapping out an action plan that matches those resources – income, savings, retirement accounts, and property – to the needs outlined over both the short and long term. This kind of planning can be incredibly helpful to people in all social and economic levels, but for practical purposes, it is available only to those people who have the means to pay planning fees ranging from perhaps $75 or $100 per hour on the low side, to as much as several hundred dollars per hour. As is even more common, those having assets of sufficient quantity to generate ongoing management fees or up-front commissions that make them attractive to traditional advisors are offered the planning service free of charge. Not only is planning readily available to these individuals and families, but there is significant competition among traditional advisors for the ready supply of prospective planning clients.

Chapter Eleven
Life Transition-Financial Maintenance

At some point your needs will change from those of a person escaping, then surviving domestic abuse, to a person once again ready to assume a fully active place in society. There are critical stages that make it possible to undergo this kind of change, and the first of these has nothing to do with managing money or time – it has to do with managing your brain. In his book, "Think and Grow Rich", author Napoleon Hill talks about how the human mind sets the stage for the acquisition of anything we get throughout our lifetimes – the good as well as the bad. It is referred to as the "Law of Attraction". You may hear people joke that you need to "watch out what you wish for, you just might get it"….it all comes from that same Law of Attraction, only the Law says you WILL get what you wish for – or put foremost in your mind – whatever it may be.

There is a way you can begin this process of change and attraction of the things you WANT in your life (see, eventually you get to do the "wants" along with the "needs"). Your mind has been focused solely on those things you had to have in order to survive, but the next step is to expand thinking beyond basic survival. Like a child learning to take its first steps, the process requires two things, practice and patience. Children never learn to walk without learning first to stand, then balance without holding on, then walking while they hold on, then finally (and with plenty of spills along the way) walking.

As a first lesson, focus your thoughts on something you really *want* – not so big that you have a hard time believing you will have it….these are our baby steps. Maybe a new item of clothing, a computer, or even a class you want to take to train you for a better job. Whatever it is, practice two or three times each day for five to ten minutes seeing yourself already possessing it. Make the vision as clear and detailed as you possibly can. Some people will need more practice than others, but keep trying…it *will* happen!

There is a fascinating process that begins to happen when we learn to control our thoughts for positive purposes: First, we begin to experience more positive things in our lives. Second, and even more important is that we begin to FEEL more confident that we are "on the right track", and those feelings create the third, and perhaps *most* important element of all, which manifest themselves in positive ACTIONS. We begin to live our lives based on the belief we now hold inside ourselves that we *deserve* all the good things coming our way, and guess what? *We get them*!

The reason it is so important to practice the way we control our thoughts is the one element hidden to most when it comes to this process of change. A crew that pours a concrete driveway – a surface hard and nearly impenetrable – takes the time to seal it against weather – something we may never even be aware of just looking at it – and the simple process of sealing expands the life of the concrete many times what it would be without it! In the same way, you seal the hard work you've done by practicing until it becomes a HABIT. Once you do that, you will never lose it…it will be yours forever.

Keep the process in your mind as you begin: Positive THINKING leads to positive FEELING that then leads to positive ACTIONS, which finally culminate in positive HABITS. Get ready for incredible changes in the direction your life takes….

Chapter 12
Managing Your Finances as a Survivor

At the beginning of the section on planning, we discussed those individuals and families who are the "typical planning clients", the ones financial advisors are all working so hard to find. One of the first tasks planners give their clients is for them to define their financial goals. In one sense, this is much the same – although on a much lower level – as the thought control we just covered. When you have the ability to define and focus on a goal…something you really want….something that's important to you….something that will make you feel GOOD about yourself….then you have a definite purpose for continuing to move ahead, to make your life better. This is important for more than the obvious reason. If you ever want to be in the position of helping someone *else* improve their life, you have to have your own in order. Learn to manage your life and you will grow into an advocate for every person you meet.

In the world of financial planning, there are six defined areas of planning that will touch the lives of every person at some point in their lives. The six areas include Cash Flow Management, Protection Planning, Accumulation Planning, Tax Planning, Retirement Planning and Estate Planning. We covered cash reserves and income needs in an earlier section, and those two areas are truly the foundation blocks of financial planning for every person, regardless of where they find themselves in life, but the benefits extend far beyond that of the survival mode.

Creating and maintaining a cash reserve for emergencies, opportunities and planned expenses is critical, no matter what your financial status, so never minimize the value of opportunity funds. Every person has, at one time or another, had the chance to get involved in a business venture that may have been their key to long-term financial security. Those with the discipline to build reserves are the ones who can take advantage of solid opportunities. This doesn't mean they throw money at everything that comes along, but if it is a good fit and makes sense, they put themselves in the position to reap the benefits. Those who haven't created the mind-set and habit of building cash reserves are the ones who find themselves sitting and wishing….

Protection planning is an area that is often overlooked, simply because talking about it brings to mind the possibility we may suffer some kind of loss, and being human, we tend to avoid thinking about loss. It may even seem to go against what we reviewed earlier about controlling our thinking, but what we want is a positive, realistic review of what we have and what we need to protect. As we move from victim to productive person, the first and most important consideration is how we protect our most valuable asset – our ability to earn income. Our income is the raw material that not only buys our food, pays our housing and utilities and builds our cash reserves, but it also allows us to begin accumulating the things we want that make our lives better for the long term. Add to that any of the goals you have begun to see in your mind – educating children, retiring, traveling, buying a home, and you will begin to see how important your income is to you and all those you care for.

Protecting your own income is the first step, and that can mean two things: If you need to have some portion of your income continue for someone else if you died, you need to own life insurance. If you need to have your income continue in the event of your own sickness or injury (beyond what your cash reserve can cover), then you need accident or disability income insurance. We won't go into the specifics of what kind or how much – that is a discussion you will need to have with an insurance professional. Just be aware that, second only to cash management, protection is the most critical area to address.

Once the cash reserve and protection areas are addressed, next on the list comes accumulation planning. Simply stated, this encompasses building your savings from whatever surplus your monthly income allows. Accumulating money can take place over any period of time, from a few months to many years. Building your cash reserve is the first type of accumulation planning you will do. Allowing money to build in a checking or savings account is the simplest way to do it, but you can also set up an automatic account withdrawal to move money out of a checking or savings account each month into some other type of account more appropriate to building long-term value.

Here we need to take a step back and talk about the types of accounts that fit your accumulation goal. There are two general types of savings plans, those that use fixed income and those that use equities. Think of fixed income as a loan. You loan money to someone and they pay you back over time. A cost to the borrower for having the use of your money is that they pay you interest along with the return of your funds. The loan usually states exactly what you will be paid over what period of time – a *fixed return*. Fixed assets are great for short-term accumulation goals. They have little or no risk to the account, only the risk that the earnings will almost always be low (remember…return OF your money, not return ON your money).

Equity assets are so named because anything in this asset class implies *ownership*. When you own an asset, you take on an additional risk that its value may go up or down, so it is more appropriate for long term accumulation goals. Equity assets can be real estate, stocks, or stock-based funds, often known as mutual funds. The advantage is that you, the owner, get to share in all the gains the asset provides, so over the long term you should come out ahead of the individual putting money into a fixed asset. You also share in all the losses, so once again, get some quality advice when choosing an equity asset for your accumulation goal.

To recap, when it comes to managing your financial life once you have escaped an abusive domestic relationship, the first and most critical element is to monitor your cash reserves and your cash flow – what comes in and what goes out every month. Next comes protecting your ability to continue bringing in income (not your *stuff* – your *income*….protect your stuff only after income protection has been addressed). Finally, manage the surplus you have and use it to save for those goals you begin to create for yourself….then create more goals! The purpose of creating goals is to make you happy and give you direction, so have fun with it!

Over time, you will need to manage the remaining three areas of your planning. Tax planning will be important for you, as proper planning will allow you to keep as much of the money you make as possible. Retirement planning will allow you to make the transition from you at work to your money at work, so you won't be one of the many people in their 70's who have to memorize the phrase, "would you like fries with that?" Finally, estate planning will allow you to make sure the assets you don't live long enough to enjoy will pass to your family the way you had intended. We all laugh at the person who says they fully intend to spend their last dime as they take their last breath, but it definitely doesn't work like that. You either come up short, or you have something extra. If you've done a good job with your planning and have that something extra to pass along – whether it's going to family, a charity, or some special cause you support, there is no reason you have to let your wishes die along with you.

Perhaps the most important message of this book is to give you the understanding that you can be an instrument for change, no matter what you have experienced in your life. You can be the one who breaks the cycle of domestic violence and abuse, and the one who creates a whole new cycle of personal and financial strength. Planning and managing your finances can be incredibly rewarding, and it is a lifetime responsibility that can have a positive effect for generations, so embrace the changes you are facing now, and know that your life will be whatever you want it to be.

Chapter 14
Life Transition – Physical Safety

The most important thing about a life transition is finding a new place in the world. Making a move from the familiar to the unknown can be emotionally exhausting and scary. First and foremost are safety issues.

Once the decision for a clean break is made and either you or the abuser relocate, some common sense issues come into play. If you remain in the previously shared home you can take the following steps:

*Change the locks- ALL the locks - and do not give out keys to anyone for the first six weeks or so. If you work, make arrangements for your children to be cared for until you arrive home.

*Arrange transportation for your children to and from school or whenever possible, change schools.

*Change your phone numbers- ALL the numbers – home phone, cell phone, and internet phone such as Magic Jack, Vonage and Google Voice.

*Invest in a program to "cloak your ISP and protect computer communications.

*Install a security system.

*Buy a dog. If you had one before you left the abusive environment it will be useless to you for protection in your new environment as it is fully acquainted with your abuser.

*If you must talk to your abuser do it via an Internet chat that archives the conversations. Copy and paste them and save them to disc for future reference.

*Take several pictures of the inside and outside of your home at least once a month.

*Create a safety plan, discuss it with your children once a week and stress the importance of not discussing it with

ANYONE including the abusive parent. Do NOT post it in your house.

*If possible, alter the route you take home but do not make it routine such as north, west and then east on Monday, Wednesdays and Fridays only.

*Buy a cell phone car charger and keep your phone charged at all times.

*Use discretion when notifying neighbors of your situation. Remember, most couples have mutual friends, some of whom may not like being "put in the middle of a mess".

*If you attend church, notify your pastor, priest, or Imam of your situation.

*Install a mail slot for letter delivery and have bulky packages delivered elsewhere.

*Learn to keep a journal complete with photographs of any incident or inadvertent contact with your abuser.

*If you live in an apartment complex, explain the situation to the building manager and make arrangements to move to another apartment as soon as one becomes available.

*If you relocate to another neighborhood, learn the “lay of the land” as soon as possible. Make a trip to the nearest police station; introduce yourself and your situation to establish credibility.

You may feel like a prisoner for the first few weeks but in reality you are a relocated survivor of domestic violence.

Chapter Fifteen
Life Transition-Emotional Wellness

Part and parcel of maintaining a success identity is creating emotional comfort zones. For most victims of domestic violence, this is the first opportunity they have had to regain any sense of self. Now that physical safety has been established it is time to deal with the psychological aftermath.

Recovery from trauma takes time and it is done in steps. For survivors to manage their new lives and thrive, it all begins with openness to the experience of life away from your abuser. This is especially true of long term ongoing abuse. Along with this openness comes the realization that you are now in total control of your own life and/or the lives of your children.

In reclaiming control, it is important to remember that this is a behavior change that must be accompanied by a change in feelings – the way you feel about yourself and your new situation. Social re-engagement, a new found sense of self respect, heightened self-esteem and personal validation lead to a feeling of empowerment.

Most victims of domestic violence have experienced conditioned fear. As a survivor it is necessary to become acclimated to the fact that the prior threat of ongoing or cyclical physical violence and/or verbal abuse is no longer a part of their daily routine.

The reason domestic violence is so traumatic is it is such an egregious breach of trust because the pain is inflicted by the people we love, respect and who in many cases are entrusted with our wellbeing such as parents, intimate partners, children, other close relatives, or frequent visitors to a household. Survivors begin to question and suspect even the smallest act of benevolence from strangers - even the helping professionals trying to assist them in their recovery. They also begin to question their ability to judge character.

As a survivor it is imperative to create a new mindset and realize that every man or every woman is not an angry abusive person and that part of your new openness and success identity is judging everyone on his or her own merits. Paranoia has no place in managing your new life.

Survivors of domestic violence experience a myriad of anger issues - self-loathing for "taking it" and remaining in the situation for so long; anger at their abuser for inflicting emotional and physical pain and anger at a societal structure that seems to minimize the impact of domestic violence by whispering it as a cause whether than roaring about it.

Managing life after the violence ends includes a strong belief in self with positive self-talk, believing you are a good person, buying into the power of the here and now. To avoid falling back into a negative identity and revisiting the past, remind yourself on a daily basis of how far you've come and begin to create a list of specific areas of change and growth. Realize and understand that it really is okay to feel good about yourself and the fact that you are a survivor.

Chapter 16- Life Transition- The Legalities

When relationships come to an end, oftentimes one partner is not so willing to go gently into that good night. The eminent loss of a partner may make a verbally or psychologically abusive partner violent, resorting to stalking and outright physical confrontations.

A big part of an exit strategy is severing ties. This means taking definitive steps to end the abusive relationship. While a restraining order or order of protection may be in force, there is little that can be done to enforce it except to report every violation to the local police. This does not mean that the legal system can't work for you. It simply means that once you initiate legal action, it is imperative that you follow through and stay the course.

In some states a temporary order of protection can be obtained even if no actual physical violence has occurred. In other states once the abusive person is arrested the process begins. To learn more about your rights in your state go to: http://www.aardvarc.org/dv/orders.shtml/

Many abusers will express guilt and ask for forgiveness in an attempt to draw you back into the abusive situation. If this happens, seek the advice of a mental health practitioner with experience in domestic violence issues.

With each step in the legal process it becomes more important to create a support safety net. The police cannot be everywhere, but you can take steps to increase their effectiveness by adhering to the rules of the order of protection. The language in the order of protection is binding on all parties.

Beyond the order of protection there is the next step to protect yourself and that is a legal separation. The purpose of this action is to generate an order of the court that determines and highlights each party's rights and responsibilities while maintaining separate residences. It should be considered a prelude to a divorce as on most occasions the language in the legal separation is incorporated into the final divorce decree. Some of the issues addressed in a separation agreement are division of assets and debts, child custody and child support, and spousal support.

Remember your abuser will most likely want visitation as a back door method of once again getting close. You have the right to request supervised visitation at a secure location with a representative from your local Department of Family Services in attendance throughout the visitation.

Suffice it to say you will need an attorney to initiate the process and assist you at all levels of dismantling your relationship. This holds true for marriages, domestic partnerships and couple cohabitating and the parents of any and all children born as a result of the relationship.

Just as making a physical transition from the abusive environment to safe space was done in steps, so is the process of selecting an attorney. The first step is creating an interview questionnaire which is simply a list of important questions to insure a quality attorney/client fit. Remember - the attorney works for you!

A good starting place to select an attorney is to call the bar association or ask someone in your support network for a name. You should plan on interviewing at least two or more attorneys and of course your main concern is the individual's experience and level of competency, specifically an attorney who is experienced in handling cases resulting from domestic violence situations.

Notify the attorney that you would like to ask a few questions and if he or she minds if you take notes. Don't feel the need to rush into a commitment with an attorney until you feel perfectly comfortable with the level of communication between you.

The following is a sample of questions you may want to ask:

*What percentage of client load is dedicated to family practice?

*What percentages of cases go to trial?

*Do you encourage mediation?

*Do you accept emergency phone calls?

*Total cost estimate

*Will you personally handle the case?

*Amount of client involvement in strategy planning.

*What will be the first actions taken in my behalf?

*How interested are you in taking my case?

*Can you get started immediately?

There are of course questions you should ask yourself after the interview before you make a commitment to an attorney to handle your case. These are:

*How comfortable do I feel having this attorney represent my interests?

*Do I feel that this attorney will communicate with me at all stages of the process?

*Will he/she be a fully engaged advocate for me?

Once you decide on an attorney, set an appointment. Then prepare a summary of personal information of you and your children if applicable. This summary should include the full names, address, occupation if employed and employer and the dates of birth, ages, and any health issues for yourself and any children.

The effectiveness of the legal system and safety networks are only as strong as your own self-advocacy. You have made this far and you have regained control of your life. Now is the time to tie up all the loose ends and legally close the door on your abusive past.

Marsha Dean Walker and James E. Eastwood

Afterword

This book was written as a guide to help the victims of abuse become the survivors of abuse. The decision to leave an abusive relationship is often fraught with more terror than anticipating and living through the abuse.

Leaving the known to venture out into the unknown alone is traumatic but when you have a strategy, the transition is safer and smoother. It fosters your confidence and independence and is reinforced by your new success identity.

As relationship and financial coaches, we have attempted to provide you with the tools to become fiscally responsible and emotionally in control of your own life. At times it may seem as if you are alone, but you are never really alone. There are countless numbers of people- helping professionals, financial professionals, support safety networks, law enforcement personnel and the courts that advocate for you.

It took a giant leap of faith in yourself to follow through with the entire process and hopefully this book has provided you a roadmap to guide you on the path to a safe and independent life - free of any abusive situation. So to you we now say

"L' Chaim!" (To life).

Appendix

The purpose of these pages is to emphasize key points in developing a strategy that takes someone from being a victim of domestic violence to a survivor of domestic violence.

It is our full intent to assist you in creating a "map" that leads from a life of abuse and victimization to a life of safety, independence and the successful transition to survivor.

Just was with most tasks getting started is the hardest part. In the thinking stage of mapping out an exit strategy many victims continually weigh whether they are really being abused or if their partner is just "going through a bad patch", or they, as the victim did something to justify the actions. Being in denial does not obliterate the general warning signs of domestic violence.

As a partner in a relationship think:

- How many hoops are you willing to jump through to please your partner into NOT hitting you or not berating you?

- How often do you cave in and go along with his or her wishes just to have peace?
- How you feel the need for your partner to know where you are and what you are doing every minute of the day for fear of a confrontation at the end of the day?
- Do you discuss your partner's temperament including obsessive and possessive behavior with other people?
- Do you get frequent or threatening calls throughout the day inquiring about your whereabouts?
- How many times have you lied about an obvious physical injury?
- How many times have you skipped work, school or social events because you suddenly developed a cold, or the flu or a migraine?
- How often have you worn long sleeved shirts in the summer or a scarf to hide injuries resulting

from a physical altercation with your significant other or applied extra layers of make-up to hide fresh wounds?

- Are you denied access to the family funds or credit cards?
- Do you have a strict curfew after work or school? Are you denied access to transportation?
- Have you ever been forbidden to interact with family members or your friends?
- Have you ever been locked in the basement, attic or garage?
- Do you suffer from low self esteem and the inability to assert yourself?
- Have you undergone a major change in personality from being independent and exuding self-confidence to someone who is now experiencing chronic fatigue, anxiety, depression and thoughts of suicide?

Thinking Stage Questionnaire

The purposes of this questionnaire are reflection, clarification, interpreting and evaluating your situation in response to the above bulleted questions.

1. How much attention do you pay to the tone of voice and posturing of your abuser during an "event"?

    a. I pay close attention.
    b. I try to tune out.
    c. It doesn't matter.

2. How sensitive are you to non-verbal messages such as disapproving looks, the silent treatment, etc.

    a. Very.
    b. Somewhat.
    c. Not at all.
    d. It doesn't matter.

3. Are you able to reflect without becoming angry, sad or engaging in negative self-talk?

    a. Yes, always.
    b. Yes, sometimes

   c. Not at all.
   d. It doesn't matter.

4. Do your reflections fully explore your true feelings about your situation?

   a. Yes.
   b. Yes, somewhat.
   c. Not at all.
   d. It doesn't matter.

5. How well do you understand that no matter what you do it will have no impact on the behavior of your abuser?

   a. I understand but I still think there is a chance things will change.
   b. I fully understand that I cannot change another person.
   c. I don't understand how a person can just change so much.
   d. It doesn't matter and I try not to think about it.

6. Are you able to identify with others in your situation or do you feel your situation is unique?

a. I definitely can identify and empathize with others in my situation.
b. I cannot identify at all because I am not like them.
c. I think my situation is unique.
d. I don't care about what anyone else is going through.

7. To what degree are you motivated to consider mapping out an exit strategy to leave your current situation?

a. Very.
b. Somewhat.
c. I think about it every now and then.
d. No, I just think things are hopeless.

Using the following coding system next to each statement write the number of the response that most accurately reflects your viewpoint:

5 = I *strongly agree* with the statement.
4 = I *agree*, in most respects with the statement.
3 = I am *undecided* in my opinion about the statement.
2 = I *disagree,* in most respects with this statement.

1 = I *strongly disagree* with this statement.

_____1. I think it is absolutely necessary to have some kind of plan before you try to leave an abusive situation.
_____2. If at all possible I would take advantage of any resource that would help me make a safe transition from victim to survivor.
_____3. Confidentiality is one issue that is of great concern to me when I think about leaving my abusive situation.
_____4. Under the right circumstances I would engage in a fair degree of self-disclosure in seeking help.
_____5. In general there are more advantages than disadvantages in striking out on my own.
_____6. I feel stupid for letting things go this far.
_____7. I am terrified of change of any sort.
_____8. I worry a lot that I need to prove myself.
_____9. I worry a lot about being able to survive on my own.
_____10. I don't think anyone can help me with my situation.

Section 2: The Planning Stage

Now that your thoughts have been organized and you feel comfortable in the knowledge that it is time to truly map out an exit strategy. The first and foremost consideration is your safety and the safety of your children if you have any. Establishing trust is key during the planning stage as you will need the help of others to make the transition from victim to survivor. There will be periods during this stage where you feel as if you have hit an emotional wall; that it all seems too much, too overwhelming. This is the time you need to find a quiet place with a pad and a pen and draw your wall. Ask yourself how high is the wall? How wide is the wall? Does the wall cloud your vision of the future? Is there a window in the wall or some way to get on the other side?

Your decision to leave is a self directed intervention with a clearly defined rationale. The goals and objectives have been clearly laid out and now it is time to implement the transition stage of the strategy. This is the time when you:

- Reject any outside attempts to keep you in your abusive relationship.
- Accept the reality that you can take control of your own life.
- Learn how to work through internal conflict.
- Recognize your resistance to change, although you know it has to happen to move away from the toxic environment.

Meet the Author

Marsha Dean Walker, MSHS, HS-BCP

A relationship coach, founding human services board certified practitioner and counselor since 1989. A graduate of Post University, Marsha Dean Walker provides coaching and mediation services for couples in individual, group, and retreat settings, as well as conducting web-based e-learning programs. Coaching services range from adult and teen domestic violence issues to motivation analysis to coaching employees in the workplace on issues affecting workplace productivity and anger management programs. She is a survivor of domestic violence.

Meet the Author

James E. Eastwood, CIS, CFP®

James Eastwood joined M. Dean Walker & Associates in 2010, and brings 24 years of experience in the financial services industry, including training as a financial advisor, Certified Investment Specialist, and CERTIFIED FINANCIAL PLANNER™, as well as his background as a life and health insurance agent, investment advisor representative, and general securities representative. He has had over 20 years experience as workshop facilitator and speaker, including presentations to corporations, unions, and community groups throughout Ohio and the surrounding areas.

Notes

Notes

Notes

www.ingramcontent.com/pod-product-compliance
Lightning Source LLC
Chambersburg PA
CBHW061751020426
42331CB00006B/1428

* 9 7 8 0 9 7 9 3 1 7 1 3 2 *